Essential Business Skills

Mastering the Tools and Strategies for Achieving Success

Wills Tom

Table of contents

Introduction

In today's fast-paced and competitive business environment, having essential business skills is critical to your success. Whether you're an entrepreneur looking to launch a startup, a manager looking to lead a team, or a seasoned professional looking to advance your career, the ability to navigate the complexities of the modern business environment is essential. is. From effective communication to strategic planning, mastering the tools and strategies that drive success in the business world will help you stand out from the competition and reach your goals.

This guide will teach you the basic business skills you need to succeed in today's economy. Leveraging the expertise of executives, entrepreneurs, and professionals in a variety of industries, we provide actionable tips, actionable advice, and real-life examples to help you master the tools and strategies you need to succeed. Whether you want to improve your communication skills, improve your leadership skills, or deepen your understanding of financial management, this guide will give you the knowledge and tools you need to take your career to the next level.

Start by exploring the fundamental skills that are the foundation for success in any business environment. From effective communication and problem-solving to time management and teamwork, these skills are essential for anyone looking to succeed in the modern workplace. We then dive deep into the specific skills and strategies required for success in various business areas, from marketing and sales to finance and operations.

This guide emphasizes the importance of hands-on application and provides concrete examples of how these skills can be applied in real-world scenarios. It also provides tools and resources for continuous learning and development beyond the scope of this guide. Whether you're a fresh graduate entering the workforce or a seasoned professional looking to stay ahead of the curve, mastering basic business skills are critical to success in today's economy. By following the advice and strategies outlined in this guide, you will be well-prepared to face the challenges and opportunities of today's business environment and achieve your goals.

Communication Skills:

Master The Art Of Effective Communication

Chapter 1:
Introduction To Effective Communication

Effective communication is a key skill that helps individuals achieve their personal and professional goals. Whether you're a student, employee, business owner, or simply looking to improve your relationships with others, mastering the art of communication can make a big difference in your life. This chapter explores what effective communication is, why it is important, and how it can be learned and practiced.

Section 1:
Understanding effective communication

Effective communication is the process of exchanging information and ideas between two or more people in a clear, concise, and understandable manner. This includes sending messages, receiving feedback, and making adjustments to ensure that messages are received and understood as intended. Effective communication is more than just speaking and writing well. It also requires active listening, empathy, and the ability to connect with others.

Effective communication is essential in every field. In the workplace, effective communication increases productivity, collaboration, and teamwork. In personal relationships, it can increase trust, understanding, and intimacy. In academic settings, effective communication can improve learning and academic performance. Essentially, effective communication can improve the quality of our lives in all aspects.

Section 2:
Why Effective Communication Matters

Poor communication can lead to misunderstandings, conflicts, and frustration. When communication breaks down, people can become defensive, hostile, or simply drop out of the conversation. Poor communication in the workplace can lead to lost productivity, missed deadlines, and costly mistakes. In personal relationships, this can lead to mistrust, resentment, and ultimately the breakdown of the relationship.

Effective communication, on the other hand, can lead to better results, both professionally and personally. You can build stronger relationships, increase productivity and efficiency, and achieve greater success in achieving your goals.

Section 3:

Elements of effective communication

Effective Communication Includes Several Key Elements, Including:

1. Clarity:
The message should be clear and simple for the recipient to understand.

2. Simplicity:
Your message should be concise and to the point, avoiding unnecessary information and details.

3. Listening:
Effective communication requires active listening. This means that you should pay attention to what the other person is saying and respond appropriately.

4. Feedback:
Feedback is an essential component of effective communication because it helps ensure that your message was received and understood as intended.

5. sympathy:
Effective communication requires empathy. Empathy means understanding and sharing the feelings of others.

Section 4:
Learn and practice effective communication

Effective communication is a skill that can be learned and practiced. Use these tips to improve your communication skills.

1. Active listening practice:
Pay attention to what others say and respond appropriately.

2. Use clear and concise language:
Use language that is easy to understand and avoid jargon and jargon that others may be unfamiliar with.

3. Practice empathy:
Try to understand the other person's point of view and feelings.

4. Send us your feedback:
Ask for feedback to make sure the message was received and understood as intended.

5. Be open-minded:
Be open to different perspectives and ideas.
Look for opportunities to practice.

Join public speaking groups, attend networking events, and converse with people from different backgrounds and cultures.

Conclusion

Effective communication is an essential skill that can improve all aspects of our lives. Whether you're a student, employee, business owner, or simply looking to improve your relationships with others, mastering the art of communication can make a big difference in your life. This chapter has explored what effective communication is, why it is important, and how it can be learned and practiced. Subsequent chapters detail specific communication skills and techniques that will help you become a more effective communicator.

Leadership Skills: Leading Teams To Success

Chapter 2:
Effective Communication For Executives

Effective communication is a key leadership skill that determines your team's success. As a leader, you need to be able to communicate clearly and effectively with team members to ensure everyone is on the same page and understands their roles and responsibilities.

One of the most important aspects of effective communication is active listening. This means participating fully in the conversation, paying attention to what the other person is saying, and trying to understand the other person's point of view. Active listening shows that you respect the opinions and ideas of your team members and helps build trust and respect. In addition to active listening, effective communication also requires clear and concise language. As a leader, you should aim to communicate in a way that everyone can understand. Avoid overly technical language and jargon that can confuse team members. Instead, break down complex ideas into simpler words and provide examples or illustrations to convey your message.

Another important aspect of effective communication is the ability to adapt your communication style to different situations and personalities. Some team members prefer a more direct style of communication, while others prefer a more collaborative approach. As a leader, it is your responsibility to recognize these differences and adjust your communication style accordingly.

Finally, effective communication requires regular feedback and check-ins. As a leader, it's important to provide regular feedback to your team members. This feedback should be specific, timely, and focused on both strengths and areas for improvement. Regular check-ins help identify problems and challenges early and keep everyone working toward the same goals.

In summary, effective communication is a key leadership skill that helps build trust, respect, and success within your team. Practice active listening, use clear and concise language, adapt your communication style to different situations and personalities, and provide regular feedback and check-ins to keep your team working towards a common goal. can confirm that there is

Time Management: Maximizing Productivity And Efficiency

Chapter 3:
Effective Time Management Strategies

Effective time management is essential for executives looking to maximize productivity and efficiency. In today's fast-paced world, there is always more work to do, and it can be difficult to juggle multiple tasks and responsibilities. However, implementing some simple strategies for effective time management can help you prioritize your work and stay focused on achieving your goals.

One of the most important strategies for effective time management is setting clear priorities. As a leader, it is your responsibility to identify the most important tasks and ensure that they are given the proper attention and resources. That means you need to be able to distinguish between urgent tasks that need immediate attention and important tasks that you can plan and prioritize.

Another important strategy for effective time management is task delegation. As a leader, it can be tempting to do everything yourself, but that's not always the most efficient way. Delegating tasks to team members with the necessary skills and expertise saves time so you can focus on more important tasks and responsibilities.

Another critical aspect of effective time management is the ability to say no. As a leader, you will inevitably be presented with numerous requests for your time and attention. However, it is essential to be able to prioritize your workload and say no to requests that do not align with your goals or priorities. Learning to say no can be challenging, but it is a vital skill that will help you to stay focused and productive.

Effective time management also requires effective scheduling. As a leader, it's important to plan your time carefully and allow enough time for important tasks and responsibilities. This means that you need to estimate how long each task will take and allocate time accordingly. Having a schedule and sticking to it maximizes productivity and efficiency.

In summary, effective time management is essential for executives looking to maximize productivity and efficiency. By setting clear priorities, delegating tasks, learning to say no, and creating effective schedules, you can use your time wisely and reach your goals.

Of course, here are some additional tips and strategies for effective time management:

1. Use time-tracking tools.

Many apps and tools help you keep track of time spent on various tasks and activities. By using these tools, you can gain valuable insight into where you are spending your time and identify areas where you may be wasting your time.

2. Prioritize self-care:

Taking care of yourself is essential to staying productive and avoiding burnout. Prioritize self-care activities such as exercise, meditation, and getting enough sleep.

3. Stack similar tasks.

Grouping similar tasks can help you stay focused and maximize your efficiency. For example, you can schedule all your meetings on his day of the week, or group all your email replies into one block of time.

4. Use the Pomodoro Technique:

The Pomodoro Technique is a time management method that involves 25 minutes of focused work followed by short breaks. This technique helps you stay focused and productive while avoiding burnout.

5. Take regular breaks:

Regular breaks are important to maintain energy and focus. Take short breaks about every hour and use them for stretching, walking, etc. to recharge your battery.

By following these tips and strategies, you can manage your time and maximize your productivity and efficiency. Remember, effective time management is not about working harder or longer, but about working smarter and more efficiently. By prioritizing your time and focusing on your goals, you can achieve great things as a leader.

Strategic Thinking: Developing A Long-term Vision For Your Busines

Chapter 4:
Developing Strategic Thinking Skills For Long-term Business Success

One of your most important tasks as a manager is developing a long-term vision for your company. Strategic thinking includes the ability to analyze complex problems, identify opportunities, and develop effective solutions that help achieve goals. This chapter explores some of the key strategies and techniques you can use to develop your strategic thinking skills and create a long-term vision for your business.

1. Define your vision and mission
To develop a long-term vision for your company, you must first define your vision and mission. A vision should outline your ideal future state, and a mission should outline your purpose and core values. Defining your vision and mission gives your company a clear direction and aligns everyone in your organization toward the same goals.

2. Do a SWOT analysis
Conducting a SWOT analysis can provide valuable insight into your business and identify areas for

improvement. This information can then be used to develop a strategic plan that leverages strengths and opportunities while addressing weaknesses and threats.

3. Identify trends and patterns

To create a long-term vision for your business, you need to be able to identify the trends and patterns that are shaping your industry. This requires keeping up with the latest trends and understanding how they may impact your business in the future. By identifying trends and patterns, you can anticipate industry changes and develop strategies to stay ahead of the curve.

4. Develop multiple scenarios

By creating multiple scenarios, you can anticipate potential challenges and opportunities and prepare accordingly. By considering different scenarios, you can gain a more comprehensive understanding of your company's risks and opportunities and develop strategic plans that can flexibly adapt to changing conditions.

5. Build a strong team

Creating a long-term vision for your business requires building a strong team that can effectively execute your strategy. That means recruiting and retaining top talent, fostering a culture of innovation and collaboration, and giving teams the resources and support they need to succeed.

6. Measure progress

To make sure you're making progress toward your long-term vision, you need to measure your performance regularly. This requires setting specific, measurable goals and tracking progress toward those goals. By monitoring your performance, you can identify areas that need adjustment and stay on track to meet your long-term goals.

Other Tips To Consider Are As Follows:

1. Foster a culture of innovation

Innovation is the key to long-term success in any business. To foster a culture of innovation, teams must be encouraged to think creatively and take calculated risks. To do that, we need to create a safe and collaborative environment where teams feel comfortable sharing ideas and experimenting with new approaches.

2. Collaborate with other users

Collaboration is essential to developing effective strategies to address complex challenges. Collaborating with others gives us different perspectives and insights that help us build more comprehensive and robust solutions. This requires building strong relationships with stakeholders, including customers, suppliers, partners, and other industry experts.

3. Stay ahead of the curve

To stay ahead of the curve, you need to stay abreast of the latest trends and developments in your industry. This requires continuous learning and development, and a willingness to try new approaches and ideas. Staying ahead of the curve allows us to anticipate industry changes and develop strategies to take advantage of them.

4. Manage risk effectively

Effective risk management is essential to developing a long-term vision for your business. This requires identifying potential risks and developing strategies to mitigate them. Effective risk management can reduce the potential for adverse consequences and create a more stable and secure business environment.

5. Effective communication

Effective communication is essential to developing and executing a long-term vision for your business. To do that, you need to communicate your vision and strategy clearly and concisely to your team, stakeholders, and customers. Through effective communication, you can build trust, inspire confidence, and keep everyone on the same page.

In summary, developing strategic thinking skills is essential to creating a long-term vision for your business. By fostering a culture of innovation, collaborating with others, staying ahead of the curve, managing risk effectively, and communicating effectively, you can create a strategic plan for long-term success. Remember, strategic thinking is an ongoing process that requires continuous learning, experimentation, and adjustment to stay ahead of the curve. Developing strategic thinking skills can help you achieve great things as a leader and drive the long-term success of your organization.

Financial Management: Managing Budgets And Making Informed Financial Decisions

Chapter 5:
Financial Management:
Manage Budgets And Make Informed
Financial Decisions

As a leader, financial management is one of the most important skills you need to master. Managing a budget and making well-informed financial decisions are essential to the success of any business, and failure to do so can lead to financial instability and failure. This chapter reviews some of the best practices and strategies for managing your budget and making informed financial decisions.

1. Understand financial reporting
To make informed financial decisions, you need to have a good understanding of financial statements. Financial statements are documents that report the financial performance of a company and include income statements, balance sheets, and cash flow statements. Understanding financial statements helps you understand the financial health of your business and make informed decisions about budgeting, investments, and other financial matters.

2. Budgeting

Creating a budget is essential to effectively manage your finances. Creating a budget helps you identify areas where you can cut costs, reduce waste, and increase revenue. A well-thought-out budget also helps you track progress and adjust your financial strategy as needed.

3. Cash flow monitoring
Cash flow monitoring is another important aspect of financial management. Cash flow refers to the flow of cash in and out of your business and is essential to having enough cash to pay your bills and invest in your business. By monitoring cash flow, you can identify potential cash flow shortfalls and take steps to mitigate them.

4. invest wisely
A wise investment is another important aspect of financial management. Investing in a business can help you grow and expand, but it also comes with risks. Making an informed investment decision requires thorough research, analysis of market trends, and weighing of risks and benefits. Investing wisely can maximize returns and minimize risks.

5. manage debt
Financial management is another important aspect of debt management. Debt can provide the necessary capital for a business, but it can also become a

significant liability if not managed properly. To effectively manage your debt, you need to develop a repayment plan, negotiate favorable terms, and avoid over-indebtedness. Managing your debt can help you avoid financial instability and maintain a healthy financial position.

6. seek professional help
Finally, seeking professional help is an effective way to manage your finances. Financial advisors, accountants, and other professionals can provide valuable insight and guidance on financial management strategies, tax planning, and other financial matters. Seeking professional help can help you make informed financial decisions and stay on track to meet your financial goals.

In summary, financial management is an essential skill for all leaders. Manage your finances effectively and develop an informed financial can make decisions. Remember that financial management requires continuous monitoring and adjustment to adapt to changes in the business environment. By mastering financial management, you can build a stable financial foundation for your business and drive long-term success.

Marketing and branding: Creating a strong brand and marketing your business effectively

Chapter 6:
Developing A Successful Brand Strategy

In the previous chapter, we discussed the importance of branding and creating a brand identity. Now consider developing a branding strategy. A brand strategy is a long-term plan outlining how a company's brand will be perceived in the market and plays an important role in building brand equity. In other words, the added value that a brand name brings to a product or service.

Developing a branding strategy requires careful planning and consideration. Here are the key steps for a successful branding strategy:

step 1:
Define your brand

The first step in developing a branding strategy is defining your brand. You need to know what your brand stands for, what it's worth, what makes it unique, and how it differs from your competitors. Your brand identity can be on your website, social media, packaging, advertising, and everything. must be consistent across channels.

Step 2:
Know your target audience

The second step is knowing your target audience. Need to understand their motivations, needs, desires, and preferences to buy your product or service? Do they know your brand? What are the pain points and how can your brand address them? By understanding your target audience, you can create a brand that resonates with them.

Step 3:
Create your brand message

The third step is to create your brand message. Your brand message should be consistent across all channels and convey your brand values and unique selling proposition. Your brand message should be clear, concise, and memorable. You need to resonate with your target audience and differentiate yourself from your competitors.

Step 4:
Create a brand identity

The fourth step is to create your brand identity. A brand identity includes a logo, color palette, typography, and imagery. Your brand identity should be consistent across all channels and reflect your brand values and personality. Your brand identity should be recognizable and memorable.

Step 5:
Increase brand awareness

The fifth step is to build brand awareness. Speak to your target audience and put your brand front and center. This can be done through advertising, public relations, events, social media, and other marketing channels. The goal is to bring excitement to the brand and get people talking about it.

Step 6:
Measure brand equity

The final step is to measure your brand equity. You need to track how your brand is perceived in the market and how it contributes to your business's success. You can measure brand equity through surveys, focus groups, and other market research methods. Creating a successful branding strategy takes time and effort, but it's worth it.

A strong brand can differentiate you from your competitors and add value to your business. Branding isn't just about creating logos and slogans. It's about connecting with your audience and building trust and loyalty.

Brand Strategy Best Practices

To ensure a successful branding strategy, follow these best practices:

1. Be authentic:
Brands must be authentic to their values.

2. Be consistent:
Your brand identity should be consistent across all channels. This includes packaging, advertising, websites, and social media.

3. Be different:
Your brand should be different from your competitors. You need a unique sales proposition that sets you apart from the competition.

4. Memorable:

Your brand identity should be memorable. You want people to remember your brand and associate it with positive emotions.

5. Engage:
Your brand should be attractive. You need to connect with your target audience and build trust and loyalty.

Sales skills: Building Relationships And Closing Deals

Chapter 7:
Master Sales Skill:
Build Relationships And Close Deals

Sales skills are essential to the success of any business. No matter how good your product or service is, if it doesn't sell, your business won't grow. This chapter covers the basic sales skills needed to build relationships and close deals.

Build A Relationship

One of the most important selling skills is building relationships with your customers. Building strong customer relationships can lead to repeat business, referrals, and a positive reputation for your business.

Tips For Building Relationships:

1. Listen to what our customers say:
Listening is key to building customer relationships. Listen to their needs, concerns, and feedback. This helps us tailor our sales approach to meet the needs of our customers.

2. Friendly:
Be friendly and open with your customers.

3. Provide added value:
We provide value beyond products and services. Share industry insights, offer helpful tips and advice, and do whatever it takes to provide excellent customer service.

4. Reliable:
Keep your promises and trust. Your customers should be able to rely on you.

5. Follow up:
Stay connected with your customers even after the sale. Follow up to make sure they are happy and to resolve any issues that may arise.

Closing The Deal

Closing a deal is the ultimate goal of a sale. Here are some sales skills that can help you close deals effectively.

1. Necessity Determination:

The first step in closing a deal is determining the customer's needs. Ask questions to understand your customer's pain points and how your product or service can help solve them.

2. Build value:
Demonstrate the value of your product or service to your customers. Describe how it will help you solve your problem or achieve your goals.

3. Objection:
Address customer objections. This may be related to price, features, or other issues. Be prepared to overcome these objections and offer solutions.

4. Create a sense of urgency:
Create a sense of urgency and encourage customers to make decisions. This may be due to limited-time offers or promotions.

5. Ask about sales:
Finally, I have a question about selling. Proceed directly with confidence. Best practices for sales skills

Here Are Some Best Practices For Mastering Sales Skills:

Do you know your product or service:
You must have a good understanding of your product or service. This will help answer any questions your customers may have and add value.

1. Active listening practice:
Active listening is essential to building customer relationships. Pay attention to what they say and answer thoughtfully.

2. Adaptable:
Every customer is different and your selling approach should be adaptable to their needs. Be flexible and be ready to adjust your approach as the situation demands.

3. Build relationships:
Building relationships with your customers can make a big difference in closing deals. Find common ground and connect with your customers.

4. Persistence:
Closing a deal requires patience. Engage with your customers, be non-intrusive and persistent.

5. Be Honest:

Honesty and transparency are essential in selling. Don't make promises you can't keep. Be open about any product or service limitations.

Conclusion

Sales skills are essential to the success of any business. Building relationships and closing deals with customers are two important sales skills that can help you grow your business. By listening, being approachable, providing value, and following up with your customers, you can build strong relationships with them. By identifying needs, creating value, addressing objections, creating a sense of urgency, and seeking to sell, you can effectively close deals. By following best practices and continuously improving your selling skills, you can:

Project Management: Planning, Executing, And Completing Projects Successfully

Chapter 8:
Project Management - Successfully Plan, Execute, And Complete Projects

Project management is the process of planning, executing, and completing a project. Skills range from planning and scheduling projects to managing team members and budgets. This chapter describes the key components of project management and best practices for successfully planning, executing, and completing projects.

Section 1:
Planned

The planning phase is the cornerstone of any successful project. This includes defining the scope of the project, identifying project goals, and outlining the project plan. Below are the key elements of the planning phase.

1. Define the scope of your project.
This includes outlining project goals, identifying outcomes, and determining project boundaries.

2. Set project goals.

Identify what the project is trying to accomplish and define clear, measurable goals to measure progress.

3. Create a project plan.
This includes creating schedules, assigning tasks to team members, and creating budgets.

4. Identify project risks.
Identify potential risks to your project, assess their likelihood and impact, and develop a risk management plan.

5. Obtain stakeholder consent:
Engage stakeholders and gain support for your project plan. This includes communicating project goals, scope, and risks.

Section 2:
Execution

Execution of the project plan includes an execution phase. Key elements of the execution phase are:

1. Communication with the team:
Keep your team informed of project status, plan changes, and emerging risks.

2. Manage project scope:
Monitor the scope of your project to ensure that it aligns with your project goals.

3. Manage project risk.
Implement a risk management plan to address risks as they arise.

4. Monitor progress.
Keep track of your project's progress, make adjustments as needed, and stay on track.

5. Manage your budget.
Monitor project costs to stay within budget.

6. Ensuring quality:
Monitor the quality of deliverables to ensure they meet project standards.

Section 3:
Completion

In the final phase, the project is completed and a smooth transition is guaranteed. Key elements of the closing phase are:

1. Confirm the completion of the project.

Ensure that all project deliverables are complete and meet project requirements.

2. Perform post-project reviews.
Review project success and identify areas for improvement.

3. Celebrate Success:
Recognize your team's efforts and celebrate successful projects.

Project Management Best Practices

To ensure successful project management, follow these best practices:

1. Involve stakeholders:
Engage stakeholders throughout the project lifecycle to ensure support and alignment with project goals.

2. Set clear expectations.
Set clear expectations about project scope, goals, timelines, and budgets.

3. Create a project plan.
Create a comprehensive project plan outlining the project scope, goals, timeline, and budget.

4. Assign roles and responsibilities.
Clearly define team member roles and responsibilities to ensure accountability and alignment with project goals.

5. Monitor progress.
Regularly monitor project progress to ensure that the project is on track and to identify any problems that may arise.

6. Deal with the problem:
Develop a risk management plan to address any issues that arise and mitigate potential risks.

7. Celebrate Success:
Recognize team members' efforts and celebrate project successes.

8. Perform post-project reviews.
Review project success and identify areas for improvement for future projects.

Conclusion

Project management is essential to the success of any project, from small to large initiatives. Effective project management includes planning, execution, and completion phases, each with important tasks. By following project management best practices, you can ensure project success and build your reputation as a top performer.

Problem-solving: Identifying And Solving Business Problems Effectively

Chapter 9:
Solution Implementation And Evaluation

After identifying and analyzing the business problem, the next step is to design and implement the solution. This chapter describes the process of implementing and evaluating solutions to effectively address identified problems. Formulation of the implementation plan

An implementation plan is a roadmap that describes the steps and resources needed to implement your solution. A well-thought-out implementation plan should include the following elements:

1. Timeline:
The timetable outlines specific dates and deadlines for each step of the implementation process.

2. Resource Allocation:
This component identifies the resources required to implement the solution. These resources include staff, budget, technology, and equipment.

3. Roles and Responsibilities:

Clearly defining the roles and responsibilities of each team member involved in the implementation process is important to ensure that everyone understands their responsibilities and takes responsibility for their actions.

4. Communication Plan:
A communication plan outlines how to inform stakeholders about the implementation process, including updates, milestones, and challenges.

5. Risk management plan:
A risk management plan describes potential risks associated with the implementation process and how to mitigate them.

Solution Implementation

The implementation process should be carried out according to the implementation plan. At this stage, it is important to monitor progress and make necessary adjustments. The following steps should be taken for a successful implementation:

1. Please notify everyone involved and make sure they are on board.
Communicate the implementation plan to all stakeholders, including employees, customers, and suppliers. Make sure they understand how your

implementation will affect them and the benefits of your solution.

2. Provide training and support:
Employees must be trained on how to use the new solution and support the transition.

3. Progress monitoring:
Continuously monitor progress against the implementation plan to ensure the project is on track. Adjust plans as needed to move the project forward.

4. Dealing with challenges:
We quickly address all challenges that arise during the implementation process. Be prepared to change your implementation plan if necessary.

5. Celebrate Success:
Celebrate milestones and achievements, maintain momentum, and involve stakeholders in the implementation process.

Solution Evaluation

After completing the implementation process, it is important to evaluate the effectiveness of the solution in addressing the identified issues. This assessment helps identify areas that need improvement and whether the solution achieved the desired results. To evaluate your solution, you should do the following:

1. Define your evaluation criteria.
Define the metrics used to judge the effectiveness of your solution. These criteria should be tied to the goals identified during the problem-resolution process.

2. We collect data:
Collect data about solution performance against defined metrics. This includes data on customer satisfaction, employee productivity, and financial performance.

3. Analyze the data.
Analyze the collected data to determine the effectiveness of the solution. Identify areas of solution improvement and unintended consequences.

4. Make adjustments.
Based on your analysis of the data, adjust your solution as needed. This may include changes in processes, procedures, or technology.

5. Communicate results:
Communicate the results of the evaluation to stakeholders. Highlight your solution's successes and improvements.

Conclusion

Developing and implementing solutions to business problems can be a daunting process, but it is essential to business success. By following the steps outlined in this chapter, organizations can be assured of implementing effective solutions that address identified issues. Evaluations are important to ensure that the solution is effective and that the organization is continuously improving its processes and procedures.

Decision-making: Making Sound Decisions For Your Business

Chapter 10:
decision Making:
Make Informed Decisions For Your Business

Making well-informed decisions is a critical aspect of running a successful business. This chapter describes the decision-making process and provides tips for making effective and informed decisions.

Decision-making Process

There are several steps in the decision-making process, and each step plays an important role in making an informed decision. These steps are:

1. Define a problem or decision.
The first step is to clearly define the problem or decision that needs to be made. This includes identifying the problem, understanding its scope, and determining the desired outcome.

2. collect information.

Once the problem is defined, the next step is to collect relevant information. This may include conducting research, consulting with experts, or collecting data.

3. Identify alternatives:
We will use the information we collect to identify some alternatives or solutions that can solve your problem.

4. Evaluate alternatives:
Evaluate each alternative based on feasibility, costs, impacts, and potential risks.

5. decide:
Select the best alternative based on the evaluation and analysis of each option.

6. Implementation decision:
Once a decision is made, an implementation plan is created and executed.

7. Decision evaluation:
Finally, evaluate your decisions to determine whether they effectively addressed the problem or achieved the desired outcome.

Tips For Fffective Decision Making

Effective decision-making requires a combination of critical thinking, strategic planning, and emotional intelligence. Here are some tips to help you make an informed decision.

1. Define your problem.
Take your time and clearly define the problem or decision you need to make. This will help you focus on finding solutions and avoiding distractions.

2. Collect relevant information:
Gather as much information as possible about the problem or decision you are making. This may include conducting research, interviewing experts, or collecting data.

3. Identify all possible alternatives:
Consider all possible alternatives or solutions to the problem.

4. Consider the impact on stakeholders:
Consider how your decisions will affect stakeholders such as employees, customers, suppliers, and shareholders.

5. Use critical thinking:

Use critical thinking to analyze the information you collect and objectively evaluate each option.

6. Ask for opinions from others:
Get input from peers, experts, or consultants for other perspectives and ideas.

7. Use your intuition:
Use your intuition and emotional intelligence to guide your decision-making process. Trust your instincts, but also balance your logical thinking.

8.Execution plan:
Develop a plan to effectively implement decisions. This may include creating schedules, allocating resources, and communicating with stakeholders. Decision evaluation:

Finally, evaluate your decisions to determine whether they effectively addressed the problem or achieved the desired outcome. Use the results of the evaluation to make adjustments for future decisions.

Conclusion

Making well-informed decisions is essential to the success of any business. By following the decision-making process and applying the tips in this chapter, you will be able to make effective and well-informed decisions to address your problems and achieve your desired results. Remember to take the time to gather relevant information, consider all possible alternatives, and objectively evaluate each option. Use your intuition and emotional intelligence to guide your decision-making process, but also balance it with logical thinking. Finally, evaluate your decisions to determine if they are effective and adjust for future decisions.

Innovation And Creativity: Generating And Implementing New Ideas

Chapter 11:
Managing Innovation Projects

Innovation projects are complex undertakings that require careful planning, execution, and oversight. Successful innovation projects require identifying and evaluating new ideas, selecting the best ones, and implementing them effectively. Innovation project management involves a combination of strategic, tactical, and operational activities aimed at creating a culture of innovation and ensuring project success. This chapter describes the key elements of managing an innovation project. First, I will explain the importance of project management and its principles. Below is an overview of the steps involved in managing an innovation project, from brainstorming to implementation. Finally, we highlight some of the challenges associated with managing innovation projects and suggest strategies for overcoming them.

Importance Of Project Management

Project management is critical to the success of any innovation project. It provides a framework for organizing, planning, and executing complex tasks to ensure projects are completed on time, within budget, and to required quality standards. Effective project management requires a combination of skills, knowledge, tools, and techniques that enable project managers to achieve project goals while managing risks and stakeholders.

Several project management principles are relevant to managing innovation projects. These principles include:

1. Define project goals.
Project goals should be clear, measurable, and aligned with organizational goals.

2. Planning:
Planning involves creating a detailed project plan that includes tasks, schedules, resources, and budgets. This includes identifying potential risks and developing risk management strategies.

3. Organization:
The organization includes identifying roles and responsibilities for project team members, establishing communication channels, and creating a project governance structure. 4th run:
Execution includes implementing the project plan, monitoring progress, and making any necessary adjustments.

5. Monitoring and Control:
Monitoring and control include tracking project progress, identifying deviations, and taking corrective action when necessary.

6. close:
Conclusions include finalizing project results, evaluating project results, and documenting lessons learned.

Innovation Project Management Procedures

Managing an innovation project involves a series of steps from idea generation to implementation. Below are the key steps for managing an innovation project.

1. Brainstorm:
Idea generation involves identifying new ideas that have the potential to create value for the company. This can be done through brainstorming sessions, customer feedback, market research, or internal R&D activities.

2. Idea screening:
Idea screening evaluates new ideas based on criteria such as feasibility, market potential, and alignment with company goals. This can be done through feasibility studies, market research, or concept testing.

3. Concept development:
Concept development involves refining selected ideas and developing a detailed concept outlining the features, benefits, and market potential of the product or service. This can be done through a prototype, design concept, or business plan.

4. Business analysis:
The business analysis includes a detailed analysis of the financial feasibility of a concept, including costs, revenues, and profit margins. This can be done through financial models or business plans.

5. Prototype development:
Prototyping involves creating a working model or prototype that demonstrates the features and benefits of a product or service. This can be done through the product development process or the service design process.

6. Testing and verification:
Testing and validation involve testing prototypes with potential customers and stakeholders to validate market potential, usability, and concept functionality. This can be done through user-her testing, focus-her groups, or surveys.

7. Introduction and Implementation:

Market launch and implementation involve introducing a product or service to the market and ensuring that it is successfully adopted by customers. This can be done through marketing campaigns, sales strategies, or the customer onboarding process.

Challenges In Managing Innovation Projects

Managing an innovation project can be difficult due to several factors. These factors include:

1. Uncertainty:
Innovation projects are often characterized by uncertainty as the outcome is not always predictable.

2. Risk:
Innovation projects involve risks such as market risk, technology risk, and financial risk. These risks must be effectively identified, analyzed, and managed to ensure project success.

3. Resource limits:
Innovation projects often require significant resources such as human, financial, and technical resources.

Managing these resources effectively can be difficult, especially when resources are limited.

4. Resistance to Change:
Innovation projects are often associated with change that can lead to resistance among stakeholders. Overcoming resistance to change requires effective communication, stakeholder engagement, and a change management strategy.

5. Cooperation:
Cross-functional teams, external partners, and stakeholders are often involved in innovation projects. Managing collaboration can be challenging as it requires effective communication, coordination, and conflict-resolution skills.

Strategies for Overcoming Challenges in Managing Innovation Projects

To overcome the challenges associated with managing innovation projects, companies can adopt several strategies. These strategies are:

1. Emphasis on agile project management:
Agile project management involves an iterative and flexible approach to project management that allows

rapid change. This approach is suitable for innovation projects as it allows for rapid prototyping and testing of new ideas.

2. Creating a culture of innovation:
Creating a culture of innovation requires fostering an environment that encourages creativity, experimentation, and risk-taking. This can be achieved by encouraging innovation, building cross-functional teams, and fostering open communication.

3. Develop a risk management plan:
Developing a risk management plan involves identifying, analyzing, and managing risks associated with the project. This can be achieved by developing contingency plans, developing risk mitigation strategies, and monitoring risks throughout the project lifecycle.

4. Effective communication:
Effective communication includes creating clear and concise communication channels that enable effective collaboration and stakeholder engagement. This can be achieved by establishing regular communication channels, providing feedback, and managing expectations.

5. Invest in training and development:

Investing in training and development means equipping project teams with the skills and knowledge they need to effectively manage innovation projects. This can be done through training programs, coaching, and mentoring.

Conclusion

Managing an innovation project is a complex task requiring a combination of skills, knowledge, and technology. It's about identifying new ideas, selecting the best ideas, and implementing them effectively. Managing innovation projects requires project managers to take a strategic, tactical, and operational approach to project management, emphasizing principles such as planning, organization, execution, monitoring, and control. To overcome the challenges associated with managing innovation projects, organizations can adopt strategies such as agile project management, creating a culture of innovation, developing risk management plans, effective communication, and investing in training and development... Effective management of innovation projects can help organizations build a culture of innovation and drive business success.

Networking: Building Relationships And Expanding Your Bisiness Network

Chapter 12:
Networking:
Building Relationships And Grow Your Business Network

Networking is an important skill for business people. It's about building and nurturing relationships with people who can help you achieve your business goals. A strong business network provides valuable opportunities, resources, and support to help you advance your career and grow your business. This chapter discusses the importance of networks, the benefits of building a business network, and strategies for growing your network.

Why Networking Matters

Networking is important for several reasons. First, you can build valuable relationships with people who offer new opportunities and resources. Business contacts may refer you to potential customers, suppliers, or investors, for example. Networking, in turn, helps you stay up to date on industry trends, news, and events. Attend conferences, seminars, and networking events to learn about the latest developments in your field and meet other like-minded professionals. Finally, networking helps develop personal and professional skills. By interacting with various people, you can improve your communication skills, negotiation skills, and interpersonal skills.

Benefits Of Building A Business Network

Building a business network offers several benefits. These include:

1. Possibilities:
A strong business network provides opportunities for career advancement and business growth. For example, business contacts can refer you to job openings, business opportunities, or potential clients.

2. Resources:
Business networks can provide resources such as information, advice, and support. For example, you can rely on your business network for advice on difficult decisions or assistance with specific projects.

3. Reliability:
A strong business network can increase credibility and reputation. By working with other successful and respected professionals, you can build a reputation for

yourself and establish yourself as a reliable and trustworthy business person.

4. Personal growth:
Building your business network will help you improve your personal and professional skills. Interacting with different people allows you to learn from their experiences, perspectives, and expertise.

Strategies For Expanding You Network

Expanding your business network requires a strategic approach. Here are some strategies you can use to grow your network.

1. Attend networking events.
Attend conferences, seminars, and networking events in your field. These events provide an opportunity to meet new people, learn about new trends and developments, and exchange ideas and information.

2. Join a professional association:
Join professional associations in your field. These organizations provide the opportunity to connect with other professionals, access training and development opportunities, and stay up to date on industry news and events.

3. Use social media:
Use social media platforms like LinkedIn, Twitter, and Facebook to connect with other professionals in your field. These platforms provide an opportunity to share ideas and expertise, connect with other professionals, and promote your business or personal brand.

4. Volunteer:
Volunteer with a charity, community group, or professional association. Volunteering provides an opportunity to meet new people, build relationships, and develop personal and professional skills.

5. Build relationships:
Building relationships is the key to growing your business network. Take the time to meet people, learn about their interests and goals, and find ways to help them. By building strong relationships, you build a network of people who can help you in return.

Conclusion

Networking is an important skill for business people. Building a strong business network provides valuable opportunities, resources, and support to help you achieve your business goals. Attending networking events, joining professional associations, using social media, volunteering, and building relationships can help you grow your business network and foster personal and professional growth. by accepting one

A strategic approach to networking will help you maximize the benefits of building your business network and establish yourself as a successful and respected professional in your field. Remember, networking is about building relationships, not just networking. Take the time to get to know people, show genuine interest in their work, and find ways to help them. This way, you can build a network of people willing to help you reach your goals.

Final advice:
Don't be afraid to step out of your comfort zone when it comes to networking. It can be daunting to attend a networking event or approach someone you don't know, but remember that maybe we're all in the same boat. Be confident, be yourself, and be open to new experiences and opportunities. With practice and persistence, networking can become a natural and enjoyable part of your professional life.

Summary

"Essential Business Skills:
Mastering the tools and strategies to succeed" can feel a sense of accomplishment and excitement. I learned a lot about what it takes to be successful in the business world and acquired a variety of valuable skills and strategies that will help me reach my goals. The book explores a wide range of topics, from effective communication and leadership to financial management and marketing. I learned how to identify my strengths and weaknesses, set achievable goals, and create a solid business plan. I also learned to manage time and resources effectively, build and lead successful teams, and face challenges in the business world with confidence and resilience.

Looking back on the journey taken in this book, you may find that some of the most valuable lessons were the most challenging for you. I felt that it was difficult to build a network with other people. Perhaps you had to confront your own biases and assumptions about business or learn to adapt to changing market conditions. Either way, you have proven to be a resilient and resourceful learner, willing to take risks and step outside your comfort zone in your quest for success.
But the journey isn't over yet. As we look to the future, we may face new challenges and opportunities that require us to continue to learn and grow. You may need to stay abreast of the latest trends and technologies or develop new skills to meet changing market demands.

You may also need to continue building and maintaining your professional network, or find new ways to stay motivated and inspired at work.

Whatever the future holds, one thing is clear.
You have the basic business skills you need to be successful. Master the tools and strategies that will help you reach your goals and build a successful career in the business world. You have proven that you are a competent and confident leader who can adapt to changing circumstances and overcome obstacles with grace and determination.

As you close this book, reflect on your steps and the skills and strategies you've learned along the way. Remember that business is about who you are, not just what you know.
Your values, your passions, your unique perspective on the world. So on your journey, never forget to stay true to yourself, stay curious and open-minded, and always strive for excellence in everything you do. please give me. With these essential business skills in your toolbox, the possibilities for the future are endless.